I0141099

RESTORATION
BEYOND
RECOGNITION

PASTOR DR. CLAUDINE BENJAMIN

RESTORATION BEYOND RECOGNITION. Copyright @ 2025. Pastor Dr. Claudine Benjamin. All rights reserved.

For more information or to book an event, contact:
inspiredtowinsouls@gmail.com

No part of this publication may be reproduced, stored in a retrieval system or transmitted in any form or by any means, electronic, mechanical, photocopying, recording or otherwise without the prior written permission of the author.

Published by:

Editor: Cleveland O. McLeish (Author C. Orville McLeish)

ISBN: 978-1-965635-65-0 (paperback)

Scripture quotations marked (NIV) are taken from the Holy Bible, New International Version®, NIV®. Copyright © 1973, 1978, 1984 by Biblica, Inc.™ Used by permission of Zondervan. All rights reserved worldwide.

Scripture quotations marked "KJV" are taken from the Holy Bible, King James Version (Public Domain).

ABOUT THE AUTHOR

Pastor Claudine Benjamin is a dynamic voice in this generation—boldly declaring the unchanging truth of God's Word with prophetic urgency and compassionate conviction. Called to minister to the broken, the wounded, and those stuck in cycles of discouragement, she carries a unique anointing to speak life into dead places and hope into hopeless hearts.

With a ministry rooted in restoration, deliverance, and spiritual empowerment, Pastor Claudine is known for her transparency, depth of biblical insight, and Holy Spirit-led teaching. Her life and message resonate deeply with those who have been through the fire and come out on the other side—those who know what it means to be broken but are determined not to be destroyed.

She has authored numerous impactful books on soul-winning, identity, purpose, and spiritual resilience, and she ministers to a growing global audience through conferences, mentorship, and discipleship initiatives.

Whether in the pulpit, on the page, or in one-on-one encounters, Pastor Claudine's mission remains clear: to see lives transformed, restored, and commissioned for kingdom impact. She believes that no story is too messy for redemption, no life too far gone for resurrection, and no person too broken for restoration.

Above all, she is a servant of the Most High God, committed to seeing His people healed, whole, and walking boldly in their God-ordained purpose—restored beyond recognition.

DEDICATION

This book is lovingly dedicated to every soul who has ever stood in the ashes of what once was—feeling forgotten, broken, or too far gone to be made whole again.

To the ones who cried silent tears while still showing up.

To the ones who lost years, strength, dreams, and identity.

To the ones who have heard the lie, "You'll never recover."

This book is for you.

May these pages remind you that God sees every crack, every scar, and every hidden place. And not only does He see, but He restores—deeply, powerfully, and completely. He makes all things new.

You will rise. You will be healed.

And when the hand of the Restorer finishes His work, you will walk out of the fire—restored beyond recognition.

ACKNOWLEDGMENT

I want to begin by acknowledging the One who is the Author of all restoration—my Lord and Savior, Jesus Christ. Without You, there would be no story, no healing, no reason to rise again. You reached into the wreckage of my life and rewrote my ending with grace, purpose, and fire. Every page of this book is a testimony to Your redeeming power.

To the Holy Spirit, my divine helper, who led every word and breathed life into every revelation—thank You for being my guide, comforter, and daily strength.

To my family, who have loved me through every storm and stood by me when life made no sense—your prayers, encouragement, and unwavering support are part of my restoration testimony.

To every spiritual son, daughter, reader, and follower who has shared your story, walked through your own wilderness, and chosen healing over hiding—thank you for reminding me why the work of restoration is worth it.

To every mentor, intercessor, and friend in the faith who helped me heal behind the scenes—your words, presence, and patience have helped shape who I am today.

And to the reader holding this book, I see you. More importantly, God sees you. May you find not just encouragement in these pages, but an encounter with the Restorer Himself. May your story be rewritten, your soul refreshed, and your purpose reawakened.

You were never forgotten. You were being fashioned.

TABLE OF CONTENTS

INTRODUCTION

FROM RUIN TO RADIANCE

L ife has a way of taking us through seasons that seem to strip away everything familiar, leaving us standing amid the wreckage of what once was. For some, it comes through the shattering of a dream. For others, it is the betrayal of trust, the loss of a loved one, a financial collapse, or the slow erosion of hope through years of disappointment. In these moments, the temptation to believe that all is lost is strong. Yet, the story of God's grace reminds us that ruin is not the end—it is often the soil in which His greatest work begins.

From the pages of scripture to the testimonies of the saints, we see this truth unfold. The ruins of Jerusalem became the setting for a revival under Nehemiah's leadership. The ashes of Job's losses gave way to double restoration. The weeping of Mary Magdalene at the empty tomb turned to joy when she heard her name spoken by the risen Savior. What man calls an ending, God often declares as the beginning of something glorious.

Ruin is never the final chapter for the one who places their trust in the Lord. It is the place where our human strength fails, but His strength is made perfect. It is where pride is dismantled, yet purpose is rebuilt. It is the proving ground where faith, refined in the fire, emerges radiant and unshakable. The psalmist declared, **"He lifted**

me out of the slimy pit, out of the mud and mire; He set my feet on a rock and gave me a firm place to stand" (Psalm 40:2 - NIV).

Radiance is not merely the absence of pain—it is the glory of God shining through a life that has been restored, healed, and repurposed for His kingdom. It is the beauty that emerges when the light of Christ illuminates what was once dark. It is the testimony that no matter how deep the valley, no matter how devastating the loss, His redeeming power can bring forth beauty from ashes.

This book is an invitation to walk through that transformation—to journey from the depths of despair to the heights of divine hope. Each page will challenge you to see your pain through heaven's perspective, to believe that even in your lowest moments, God's hand is at work, and to embrace the truth that your life's story is not defined by the ruins, but by the radiance He will bring from them.

By the time you finish this journey, you will be able to declare with confidence: **"The Lord has done this, and it is marvelous in our eyes." (Psalm 118:23 - NIV).**

CHAPTER 1

THE GOD WHO RESTORES

There are few themes more beautiful in scripture than that of restoration. God is not only the Creator of life, but also the Restorer of what seems hopeless, broken, and beyond repair. From the fall of man to the redemption through Christ, the Bible is a divine narrative of restoration—restoration of identity, relationship, purpose, and promise.

THE NATURE OF GOD AS RESTORER

Restoration is not merely something God does—it is who He is. Throughout scripture, we see a consistent pattern: what man ruins, God rebuilds. What sin shatters, grace redeems.

"And I will restore to you the years that the locust hath eaten..." — Joel 2:25a (KJV)

This verse is not merely poetic; it is prophetic. God speaks through the prophet Joel to a people who had suffered immense loss—loss caused by disobedience, warfare, and destruction. And yet, God's response is not to discard them but to promise restoration.

Even in the story of Job, we see this divine character revealed. Job loses everything—his children, his wealth, his health. But the final chapter doesn't end in ruin.

"And the Lord turned the captivity of Job… also the Lord gave Job twice as much as he had before." — Job 42:10 (KJV)

God's restoration went beyond possessions—it was emotional, spiritual, and relational. He restored Job's dignity, honor, and peace.

RESTORATION BEGINS WITH SURRENDER

The process of divine restoration always begins when we come to the end of ourselves. True healing begins when we admit we are broken. God cannot restore what we pretend isn't shattered. Many people walk around spiritually limping, emotionally bleeding, and mentally exhausted, yet unwilling to surrender.

"He healeth the broken in heart, and bindeth up their wounds." — Psalm 147:3 (KJV)

The Lord specializes in restoring what man discards. The bruised reed, the smoldering wick—He does not break or quench (**see Isaiah 42:3**). He is gentle with the broken, and firm with the enemy who tried to destroy us.

RESTORATION IS NOT A RETURN—IT'S A REBIRTH

Many believe restoration means simply going back to how things used to be. But God's restoration goes beyond that. He doesn't just put the pieces back together—He makes something entirely new. Your restoration won't look like your past; it will reflect your destiny.

"Behold, I will do a new thing; now it shall spring forth; shall ye not know it?" — Isaiah 43:19 (KJV)

You may come to God expecting Him to return what was lost, but He often gives something greater, something eternal. He restores joy, renews hope, and revives destiny.

GOD RESTORES PUBLICLY WHAT WAS LOST PRIVATELY

One of the most profound aspects of God's restoration is that He doesn't just do it in secret. While healing may begin in private, restoration often happens in public. This is not for our glory, but for His.

"Thou preparest a table before me in the presence of mine enemies…" — Psalm 23:5 (KJV)

God will often restore you in front of those who thought your story was over. He doesn't just bring you back—He elevates you to show the power of His grace. You will not be restored to be the same— you will be restored beyond recognition.

THERE IS NO EXPIRATION DATE ON GOD'S PROMISE

Some believe they have missed their moment. Too much time has passed, too many mistakes have been made, and too many doors have closed. But the truth is, God's timing is perfect, and His promises do not expire.

"For the gifts and calling of God are without repentance." — Romans 11:29 (KJV)

You may feel like the dream is dead. But God is the Resurrection and the Life (**see John 11:25**). If He said it, He will perform it. Restoration may not come on your schedule, but it will come on His.

REFLECTION

- Where have you seen God begin the process of restoration in your life?

- Are there areas you've deemed "too far gone" for God to redeem?

- Have you confused restoration with returning to your old life instead of embracing something new?

SCRIPTURE REFERENCES

- Joel 2:25
- Job 42:10
- Psalm 147:3
- Isaiah 42:3
- Isaiah 43:19
- Psalm 23:5
- Romans 11:29
- John 11:25

CHAPTER 2

WHEN THE BROKEN ARE REBUILT

There is a holy beauty in brokenness when it is placed in the hands of the Master Builder. God is not repelled by our shattered pieces—He is drawn to them. When man sees ruins, God sees raw material. When others see failure, God sees a future. Heaven specializes in rebuilding what has been broken beyond recognition.

BROKENNESS IS NOT THE END–IT'S THE BEGINNING

The world often treats broken things as worthless. But God views brokenness as a foundation for reconstruction. You don't have to hide the places where life has torn you apart. Those are the very places where God begins His best work.

> **"The Lord is nigh unto them that are of a broken heart; and saveth such as be of a contrite spirit." — Psalm 34:18 (KJV)**

God doesn't despise brokenness. He draws near to it. He doesn't reject those who've fallen—He lifts them up and begins a rebuilding process that will testify of His power.

GOD REBUILDS WITH INTENTION AND DETAIL

When Nehemiah returned to rebuild the walls of Jerusalem, it wasn't a random construction project—it was strategic, prayerful, and purposeful. God doesn't rebuild haphazardly. Every stone is placed with care, every section fortified with divine purpose.

> **"Then I told them of the hand of my God which was good upon me… And they said, Let us rise up and build. So they strengthened their hands for this good work." — Nehemiah 2:18 (KJV)**

Rebuilding often requires the courage to look at the damage. Nehemiah had to inspect the ruins by night before the reconstruction began (**see Nehemiah 2:13**). God may take you on a painful tour of what was broken, but only so He can rebuild it stronger.

THE FOUNDATION MUST BE RESET

Before rebuilding can truly begin, the foundation must be addressed. Many times, what caused our collapse was not the storm but the faulty foundation. That's why God sometimes allows us to break—to remove what was unstable and lay a stronger base in Him.

> **"Except the Lord build the house, they labour in vain that build it…" — Psalm 127:1 (KJV)**

Restoration isn't about reconstructing your old life on the same weak principles. It's about rebuilding your life on the unshakable foundation of Jesus Christ.

"For other foundation can no man lay than that is laid, which is Jesus Christ." — 1 Corinthians 3:11 (KJV)

REBUILDING REQUIRES PARTICIPATION

God restores, but He also invites us to partner with Him in the rebuilding process. You must be willing to pick up the tools of faith, prayer, obedience, and endurance. The rebuilding season requires discipline, discernment, and sometimes discomfort.

"And they that shall be of thee shall build the old waste places: thou shalt raise up the foundations of many generations..." — Isaiah 58:12 (KJV)

You are not just being rebuilt for yourself—you are being rebuilt for future generations. What God is doing in your life now will echo through those who come after you.

WHEN GOD REBUILDS, HE DOESN'T JUST RESTORE— HE REINFORCES

God's restoration process includes divine reinforcement. What broke you before won't break you again. What collapsed under pressure before is now strengthened with wisdom, faith, and spiritual maturity. When God rebuilds, He strengthens what remains.

"Strengthen ye the weak hands, and confirm the feeble knees." — Isaiah 35:3 (KJV)

You are not being rebuilt to be fragile. You are being fortified. Your faith will be stronger, your joy deeper, and your discernment sharper. What the enemy used to destroy you will become the very tool God uses to elevate you.

REFLECTION

- What areas of your life need to be rebuilt by God?

- Have you surrendered to the rebuilding process, or are you still mourning the ruins?

- Are you willing to let God lay a new foundation beneath your feet?

SCRIPTURE REFERENCES

- Psalm 34:18
- Nehemiah 2:13, 18
- Psalm 127:1
- 1 Corinthians 3:11
- Isaiah 58:12
- Isaiah 35:3

CHAPTER 3

FROM ASHES TO BEAUTY

Ashes are the remnants of what once was—charred remains of dreams, joy, innocence, and hope. But in God's redemptive hands, ashes are not the end. They are the beginning of beauty. What others see as destruction, God sees as the foundation for divine transformation.

THE EXCHANGE ONLY GOD CAN MAKE

One of the most powerful promises in scripture is found in Isaiah 61. This divine exchange isn't fair by human standards, but it's glorious in the economy of grace.

> **"To appoint unto them that mourn in Zion, to give unto them beauty for ashes, the oil of joy for mourning, the garment of praise for the spirit of heaviness..." — Isaiah 61:3 (KJV)**

God doesn't just remove the ashes—He replaces them. He gives beauty. He doesn't just stop the tears—He brings oil for joy. He doesn't just lift heaviness—He clothes you in praise. That is the restorative nature of our God.

ASHES SPEAK OF WHAT WAS BURNED, BUT BEAUTY SPEAKS OF WHAT WAS BORN

Ashes mean something died. But beauty in God's kingdom often arises from what's been consumed. The fire may have destroyed what you built, but it could not destroy what God purposed. What is born after the fire is more valuable than what existed before it.

"Although the fig tree shall not blossom… yet I will rejoice in the Lord, I will joy in the God of my salvation." — Habakkuk 3:17–18 (KJV)

Joy that comes after loss is a deeper joy. Praise that rises from pain is pure. Beauty that emerges from ashes is more radiant because it was shaped in the fire of suffering and the furnace of faith.

GOD TURNS MESS INTO MINISTRY

Some of the most powerful ministries are born from the ashes of personal tragedy. God takes the worst moments of our lives and uses them as launching pads for healing others. Your testimony of how you came through the fire will be the oil that anoints someone else's deliverance.

"And we know that all things work together for good to them that love God, to them who are the called according to his purpose." — Romans 8:28 (KJV)

God is not the author of tragedy, but He is the Master of redemption. He does not waste pain. He recycles it into purpose.

FROM MOURNING TO MOVEMENT

Ashes can immobilize. Loss can paralyze. But God does not leave you in mourning—He calls you to move forward. Mourning has a season, but movement is a decision. Eventually, you must rise from the ashes and embrace what God is doing next.

"...weeping may endure for a night, but joy cometh in the morning." — Psalm 30:5 (KJV)

What burned down in your life may never come back the same way. But what rises in its place will carry a divine fingerprint. Don't settle in sorrow when beauty is waiting on the other side.

BEAUTY IN THE SCARS

The marks left by the fire—the emotional, spiritual, and mental scars—are not signs of shame, but signs of survival. Scars do not say "I was defeated"; they declare, "I made it through." Even Jesus, in His glorified body, showed His scars.

"Then saith he to Thomas, Reach hither thy finger, and behold my hands... and be not faithless, but believing." — John 20:27 (KJV)

Your scars may become the very proof that restoration is real. God is not trying to erase your story. He's rewriting it with beauty, grace, and power.

REFLECTION

- What "ashes" in your life are you still mourning over?

- Are you ready to receive the beauty God wants to give in exchange?

- Can you see your past pain as the platform for your future purpose?

SCRIPTURE REFERENCES

- Isaiah 61:3
- Habakkuk 3:17–18
- Romans 8:28
- Psalm 30:5
- John 20:27

CHAPTER 4

THE POWER OF THE POTTER'S WHEEL

Brokenness in the hands of man leads to abandonment. But brokenness in the hands of the Potter leads to transformation. The Potter's wheel is not a place of punishment—it is a place of process. It is where God reshapes, refines, and restores us into vessels of purpose and honor.

THE POTTER'S SOVEREIGN CONTROL

The imagery of God as the Potter and we as the clay is both comforting and humbling. It reminds us that we are not self-made. We are crafted by divine hands that see the finished product, even when we only see the mess.

> **"But now, O Lord, thou art our father; we are the clay, and thou our potter; and we all are the work of thy hand." — Isaiah 64:8 (KJV)**

On the Potter's wheel, God is not surprised by our imperfections. He anticipates our flaws and still chooses to work with us. He doesn't discard the marred clay—He starts over with mercy.

BROKEN, BUT NOT REJECTED

Jeremiah was sent to the potter's house to receive divine revelation about Israel's condition. The clay was marred—flawed in the Potter's hand. But the Potter didn't throw it away. He remade it.

"And the vessel that he made of clay was marred in the hand of the potter: so he made it again another vessel, as seemed good to the potter to make it." — Jeremiah 18:4 (KJV)

This is God's heart toward the broken. He doesn't scrap the vessel. He reshapes it into something new, something strong, something usable. Failure is not final on the Potter's wheel. It's just the start of another formation.

THE WHEEL IS SPINNING FOR YOUR GOOD

The Potter's wheel is in constant motion, symbolizing the continual work of God in our lives. While it may feel disorienting, the spinning is not chaos—it's controlled. You may feel like your life is turning without direction, but God is shaping you with divine precision.

"Being confident of this very thing, that he which hath begun a good work in you will perform it until the day of Jesus Christ." — Philippians 1:6 (KJV)

He doesn't start shaping you and then abandon the process. Every turn of the wheel is preparing you for the next level of usefulness in His kingdom.

PRESSURE PRODUCES PURPOSE

The Potter must apply pressure to shape the clay. Without pressure, there is no form. Without stretching, there is no vessel. The pressure you're feeling isn't a sign that you're being destroyed—it's a sign you're being formed.

> **"My brethren, count it all joy when ye fall into divers temptations; Knowing this, that the trying of your faith worketh patience." — James 1:2–3 (KJV)**

God uses trials not to destroy you but to mold you. The Potter's fingers may press into your soul, but they are molding you into a vessel that can hold glory.

FROM COMMON CLAY TO CONSECRATED VESSEL

After the vessel is formed, it must be dried and then fired in the kiln to be hardened and sealed. The fire doesn't destroy the vessel—it completes it. It seals the form, strengthens the body, and prepares it for use.

> **"But we have this treasure in earthen vessels, that the excellency of the power may be of God, and not of us." — 2 Corinthians 4:7 (KJV)**

We are vessels of clay, but the treasure inside is divine. God doesn't need perfect containers. He uses surrendered ones. Once you've been through the Potter's fire, you carry something precious that can bless others.

REFLECTION

- Are you resisting the Potter's hand, or surrendering to His process?

- Can you identify the areas in your life where God is applying pressure to shape you?

- Have you accepted that being on the wheel is necessary before being used?

SCRIPTURE REFERENCES

- Isaiah 64:8
- Jeremiah 18:4
- Philippians 1:6
- James 1:2–3
- 2 Corinthians 4:7

CHAPTER 5

GRACE IN THE WILDERNESS

The wilderness is often seen as a place of emptiness, confusion, and barrenness. But in God's plan, the wilderness is not a punishment—it is a proving ground. It is a sacred place where distractions are stripped away and divine dependence is birthed. It is not where we are abandoned, but where we are encountered. And above all, it is where grace flows freely in the most unexpected ways.

THE WILDERNESS IS A PLACE OF DIVINE ENCOUNTER

Some of the most powerful revelations in scripture happened in wilderness places. Moses met God in a burning bush in the wilderness of Horeb. Israel saw God's provision and power in the desert. Jesus was led by the Spirit into the wilderness before beginning His public ministry.

"And he was there in the wilderness forty days, tempted of Satan; and was with the wild beasts; and the angels ministered unto him." — Mark 1:13 (KJV)

Though it may feel dry and desolate, the wilderness is full of divine activity. Angels minister. Lessons are learned. Character is forged. Grace is revealed.

GOD SPEAKS TENDERLY IN THE WILDERNESS

In our brokenness, God often whispers words we would not have heard in our busyness. The wilderness quiets the noise of life so we can hear the gentle voice of the Shepherd.

"Therefore, behold, I will allure her, and bring her into the wilderness, and speak comfortably unto her." — Hosea 2:14 (KJV)

God doesn't shout in the wilderness. He draws us close. He uses our solitude to restore our soul. The wilderness becomes a classroom of intimacy and a womb for rebirth.

GRACE SUSTAINS WHAT STRENGTH CANNOT

In the wilderness, our strength is exhausted, but God's grace is sufficient. You may not feel strong enough to move forward, but grace is not based on your capacity—it's based on God's sufficiency.

"And he said unto me, My grace is sufficient for thee: for my strength is made perfect in weakness..." — 2 Corinthians 12:9 (KJV)

In the wilderness, God strips us of self-reliance so that we may experience supernatural supply. You may feel like you're surviving on manna, but that manna is grace, sent fresh daily from heaven.

GOD MAKES A WAY IN THE WILDERNESS

The wilderness may appear as a place of dead ends, but God turns it into a highway of hope. He specializes in making roads where there are none and rivers where there is no rain.

> **"Behold, I will do a new thing... I will even make a way in the wilderness, and rivers in the desert." — Isaiah 43:19 (KJV)**

Even in barren places, God can birth new things. What looked like the end may be the birthplace of a new beginning. Restoration doesn't skip the wilderness—it starts there.

THE WILDERNESS IS TEMPORARY, BUT THE TRANSFORMATION IS PERMANENT

The wilderness is not the destination; it's the process. God never intended for His people to dwell in the desert forever. It's a passage, not a prison.

> **"And thou shalt remember all the way which the Lord thy God led thee these forty years in the wilderness... to humble thee, and to prove thee, to know what was in thine heart..." — Deuteronomy 8:2 (KJV)**

Wilderness seasons test us, but they also prepare us. God uses the wilderness to expose what needs healing and to prepare us for the promise that lies ahead. Grace doesn't just get us through—it changes who we are.

REFLECTION

- Have you misjudged your wilderness season as abandonment rather than preparation?

- What has God been whispering to your heart in the silence?

- Can you trace moments of grace that have sustained you, even in your driest places?

SCRIPTURE REFERENCES

- Mark 1:13
- Hosea 2:14
- 2 Corinthians 12:9
- Isaiah 43:19
- Deuteronomy 8:2

CHAPTER 6

A NEW NAME, A NEW IDENTITY

True restoration is not just about what God brings back to you—it's about who He calls you to become. In scripture, names carry meaning, identity, and destiny. When God changes your name, He's not just giving you a new label—He's releasing a new identity. He's declaring that who you were is no longer who you are.

When you've been through the fire, the wilderness, the breaking, and the reshaping, God doesn't just restore your soul—He restores your identity. You come out not only healed but renamed, redefined, and repurposed.

GOD RENAMES WHAT HE REDEEMS

All throughout scripture, when God does a deep work in a person, He gives them a new name that reflects their new purpose and destiny.

> **"Thou shalt no more be termed Forsaken... but thou shalt be called Hephzibah... for the Lord delighteth in thee..."**
> **— Isaiah 62:4 (KJV)**

What was once labeled by shame, God renames with love. What the world called you—rejected, forgotten, failure—God now calls chosen, delighted in, redeemed.

"He that hath an ear, let him hear what the Spirit saith unto the churches; To him that overcometh will I give to eat of the hidden manna, and will give him a white stone, and in the stone a new name written, which no man knoweth saving he that receiveth it." — Revelation 2:17 (KJV)

This is not just symbolic. It's spiritual. When God restores, He gives you a name heaven recognizes, even if earth doesn't yet.

JACOB TO ISRAEL: FROM DECEIVER TO DESTINY

Jacob, whose name meant "supplanter" or "deceiver," lived much of his life manipulating situations. But after wrestling with God, he was transformed—and so was his name.

"And he said, Thy name shall be called no more Jacob, but Israel: for as a prince hast thou power with God and with men, and hast prevailed." — Genesis 32:28 (KJV)

The name change was not just about identity—it was about position. Jacob went from one who grasped at blessings to one who carried divine authority. When God restores you, He doesn't just clean you up—He repositions you with favor.

ABRAM TO ABRAHAM: FROM PROMISE TO FULFILLMENT

Abram's name meant "exalted father," but God changed it to Abraham—"father of many nations"—to reflect the greater purpose He was stepping into.

"Neither shall thy name any more be called Abram, but thy name shall be Abraham; for a father of many nations have I made thee." — Genesis 17:5 (KJV)

Restoration includes redefinition. God calls you not according to where you are, but according to what He sees ahead. Even before Abraham saw the fulfillment, God gave him the name of the outcome.

FROM SIMON TO PETER: FROM INSTABILITY TO STRENGTH

Simon was impulsive, emotional, and easily shaken. But Jesus saw something more and gave him a new name—Peter, which means "rock."

"Thou art Simon the son of Jona: thou shalt be called Cephas, which is by interpretation, A stone." — John 1:42 (KJV)

God doesn't rename you based on what you've done but based on what He has destined you to do. Simon had failures ahead, including denying Jesus. But Jesus still called him "rock," showing that grace declares your destiny in advance.

YOUR IDENTITY IS IN CHRIST, NOT IN YOUR PAST

When you are restored, your identity is no longer defined by the brokenness you came out of. You are now in Christ, and that means you are brand new.

"Therefore if any man be in Christ, he is a new creature: old things are passed away; behold, all things are become new." — 2 Corinthians 5:17 (KJV)

You are not your trauma. You are not your mistake. You are not your reputation. You are who God says you are. And in Christ, you are whole, called, forgiven, loved, and chosen.

REFLECTION

- Are you still answering to names God never gave you?

- Have you embraced the identity God has declared over you?

- What name do you believe God is calling you in this new season?

SCRIPTURE REFERENCES

- Isaiah 62:4
- Revelation 2:17
- Genesis 32:28
- Genesis 17:5
- John 1:42
- 2 Corinthians 5:17

CHAPTER 7

HEALING WHAT WAS HIDDEN

Not all wounds bleed openly. Some of the deepest hurts lie buried beneath smiles, ministry titles, achievements, and daily routines. These are the wounds we've hidden from others—and often from ourselves. But restoration is incomplete until those hidden places are healed. God doesn't just deal with the visible scars. He lovingly exposes and restores what's been concealed, neglected, and forgotten.

GOD SEES WHAT OTHERS MISS

There is nothing hidden from God. He sees beyond appearances and behaviors and reaches into the depths of the human soul. The things you've buried—the abuse, betrayal, rejection, shame, or unspoken grief—are not hidden from Him.

> **"O Lord, thou hast searched me, and known me... thou understandest my thought afar off." — Psalm 139:1–2 (KJV)**

God doesn't uncover hidden pain to embarrass you—He reveals it to heal it. He is gentle, yet thorough. He knows how to reach the place where the wound was first inflicted and restore what was broken there.

HEALING BEGINS WITH EXPOSURE

Just like a surgeon must open a wound to clean it before stitching it closed, God brings hidden pain into the light so it can be fully healed. What is not revealed cannot be restored. What stays in darkness will fester, but what comes into the light is healed.

"For nothing is secret, that shall not be made manifest; neither any thing hid, that shall not be known and come abroad." — Luke 8:17 (KJV)

God's light does not condemn—it cleanses. He reveals the root of the pain so He can restore the place of the wound.

HIDDEN PAIN PRODUCES VISIBLE PATTERNS

Many of the destructive patterns in our lives—cycles of insecurity, fear, perfectionism, anger, or isolation—are the fruit of hidden wounds. We treat the behavior but ignore the brokenness beneath it. But God wants to go deeper.

"The heart is deceitful above all things, and desperately wicked: who can know it? I the Lord search the heart..." — Jeremiah 17:9–10 (KJV)

Only God can fully diagnose the condition of your heart. He doesn't just bandage the symptom; He heals the source.

JESUS HEALS THE INNER MAN

Christ did not just come to heal physical ailments—He came to restore the whole person. Emotional and internal healing are part of the redemptive package. Your soul—your mind, will, and emotions—can be made whole in Him.

"He hath sent me to bind up the brokenhearted..." — Isaiah 61:1 (KJV)

"He restoreth my soul..." — Psalm 23:3 (KJV)

No pain is too deep. No trauma is too old. No memory is too distant. God's healing reaches into the places we don't even know need healing. He restores your soul, not just your schedule or image.

GOD USES TRUTH AS THE TOOL FOR HEALING

To be healed, you must allow truth to confront your hidden areas. The truth doesn't always feel good, but it sets you free.

"And ye shall know the truth, and the truth shall make you free." — John 8:32 (KJV)

Truth is a divine scalpel—cutting not to hurt, but to heal. When you invite the Holy Spirit into the secret places, He begins to replace lies with truth, and trauma with testimony.

REFLECTION

- What areas of your life have you kept hidden, even from yourself?

- Are there patterns or habits that may be rooted in unhealed wounds?

- Will you allow the Holy Spirit to bring light into the dark places of your heart?

SCRIPTURE REFERENCES

- Psalm 139:1–2
- Luke 8:17
- Jeremiah 17:9–10
- Isaiah 61:1
- Psalm 23:3
- John 8:32

CHAPTER 8

RESTORATION IN THE PRESENCE OF ENEMIES

One of the most profound expressions of God's justice and love is His ability to restore His people publicly—in the very places where they were shamed, betrayed, rejected, or opposed. God does not always remove your enemies. Sometimes, He prepares a table right in front of them, not to humiliate them, but to vindicate His hand on your life.

Restoration is not always done in secret. There are times when God restores you in plain view of those who said you'd never recover.

A TABLE PREPARED IN THE MIDST OF OPPOSITION

David knew the sting of betrayal, the pain of pursuit, and the exhaustion of being hunted. Yet, even in that pressure, he wrote one of the most comforting truths in Psalm 23:

> **"Thou preparest a table before me in the presence of mine enemies: thou anointest my head with oil; my cup runneth over." — Psalm 23:5 (KJV)**

This is not a table of revenge—it's a table of restoration. God doesn't just rescue you; He blesses you where others said you'd break. He anoints your head not in isolation but in front of the opposition. That is divine vindication.

GOD RESTORES WHAT WAS PUBLICLY ATTACKED

When Job's character was assaulted and his life collapsed, his restoration wasn't done in the shadows. After his testing, God publicly restored him—twice as much as before.

> **"And the Lord turned the captivity of Job... also the Lord gave Job twice as much as he had before." — Job 42:10 (KJV)**

Those who watched him suffer were also witnesses to his recovery. Restoration beyond recognition means that even those who mocked your fall will see your rise.

JOSEPH: PROMOTED WHERE HE WAS PERSECUTED

Joseph was betrayed by his brothers, falsely accused, and forgotten in prison. Yet, God lifted him up—not away from his past, but in full view of the very ones who sold him out.

> **"And Pharaoh said unto Joseph, See, I have set thee over all the land of Egypt." — Genesis 41:41 (KJV)**

Later, when his brothers came needing help, Joseph had the chance to take revenge. Instead, he wept and forgave. His restoration became a blessing to the very ones who broke him.

> **"But as for you, ye thought evil against me; but God meant it unto good..." — Genesis 50:20 (KJV)**

Your enemies do not have the final word—God does. And when He restores you, He uses your story to reveal His sovereignty and mercy.

YOUR RESTORATION IS A WITNESS

Sometimes your restoration is not just for your benefit—it's for God's glory. When He restores you in the presence of those who doubted you, it becomes a testimony to the watching world.

"And all that heard them laid them up in their hearts, saying, What manner of child shall this be! And the hand of the Lord was with him." — Luke 1:66 (KJV)

When God's hand is on your life, people notice. Restoration in public places sends a message: God finishes what He starts. He exalts whom He chooses. He defends His own.

DON'T SEEK REVENGE—WAIT FOR REVELATION

It can be tempting to want justice in your own way. But restoration is not about proving people wrong—it's about proving God right. Don't fight your enemies; let God set the table.

"Dearly beloved, avenge not yourselves... for it is written, Vengeance is mine; I will repay, saith the Lord." — Romans 12:19 (KJV)

Your role is to stay faithful. His role is to restore. When you release the need for revenge, you make room for divine restoration that surpasses your expectations.

REFLECTION

- Are you still trying to prove yourself to people God has already vindicated you from?

- Can you trust God to restore you publicly without needing to retaliate?

- What would it look like for you to feast at the table He's preparing, even in the presence of enemies?

SCRIPTURE REFERENCES

- Psalm 23:5
- Job 42:10
- Genesis 41:41
- Genesis 50:20
- Luke 1:66
- Romans 12:19

CHAPTER 9

WHEN THE YEARS ARE REDEEMED

There's a kind of restoration that reaches deeper than material blessings. It's when God restores time—years that were stolen, wasted, or consumed by pain, sin, delay, or disappointment. In His mercy, God doesn't just give back what was lost—He redeems the time itself. Only the Redeemer of time can reach back into the years that felt empty and bring purpose from them.

GOD PROMISES TO RESTORE TIME, NOT JUST THINGS

One of the most powerful restoration promises in scripture speaks not only of things lost but years lost:

"And I will restore to you the years that the locust hath eaten, the cankerworm, and the caterpiller, and the palmerworm..." — Joel 2:25 (KJV)

This is divine mathematics. You can't relive the past, but God can cause the fruit, impact, and reward of those lost years to manifest in your future. What took ten years to lose can be recovered in a divine moment of favor.

NOTHING IS BEYOND GOD'S REACH

Some years feel like they vanished into thin air—years spent in addiction, toxic relationships, wilderness seasons, wrong decisions, or spiritual stagnation. But God is not limited by time. What you lost in delay, He can redeem in acceleration.

"So the last shall be first, and the first last: for many be called, but few chosen." — Matthew 20:16 (KJV)

This speaks of God's ability to reverse timelines. Your lateness in man's eyes does not disqualify you from being first in line for His favor. With God, restoration often comes with acceleration.

REDEMPTION OF TIME LOOKS LIKE FRUITFULNESS IN SHORT SEASONS

When God redeems time, He causes your fruit to multiply in ways that don't make natural sense. You'll reap where you didn't sow and receive in seasons where others are still waiting. This is not unfair—it's favor.

"And the floors shall be full of wheat, and the vats shall overflow with wine and oil." — Joel 2:24 (KJV)

The overflow is often a sign that time is being redeemed. God makes up for the dry years by releasing supernatural productivity.

THE ENEMY DOESN'T GET THE FINAL SAY OVER YOUR TIME

Satan is a thief (**see John 10:10**), and one of the greatest things he tries to steal is time—your youth, your energy, your opportunities. But he cannot override God's ability to restore and redeem.

> **"And I will restore to you the years that the locust hath eaten, the cankerworm, and the caterpiller, and the palmerworm, my great army which I sent among you." —Joel 2:25 (NIV)**

God keeps the record. He knows how to repay what was stolen. And when He does, it doesn't just look like getting things back—it looks like walking in a level of joy, peace, and maturity that was once thought impossible.

REDEEMED TIME LEADS TO REDEEMED PURPOSE

When God redeems your time, He also realigns you with your original purpose. Even if you wandered off course, He reroutes your life to intersect again with destiny. You are not behind—you are right where He wants you when you submit to His process.

> **"See then that ye walk circumspectly, not as fools, but as wise, redeeming the time, because the days are evil." — Ephesians 5:15–16 (KJV)**

You don't have to waste another moment. Every day you walk in obedience becomes a seed that grows in restored purpose.

REFLECTION

- Are there years of your life you feel were wasted?

- Have you believed the lie that it's "too late" for your calling?

- Are you willing to trust God to not only restore but also redeem the time?

SCRIPTURE REFERENCES

- Joel 2:25
- Matthew 20:16
- Joel 2:24
- John 10:10
- Ephesians 5:15–16

CHAPTER 10

LIVING RESTORED, WALKING RENEWED

Restoration is not a moment—it is a lifestyle. It's not only about what God brings you out of, but how you choose to walk afterward. Many people experience moments of breakthrough, but few learn how to maintain the renewed life that restoration births. Living restored means walking in new rhythms, renewed identity, and sustained surrender.

It's not enough to be delivered—you must decide to walk in the newness of life every day.

RESTORATION MUST BE CARRIED WITH RESPONSIBILITY

Once you've been restored, you cannot return to the same thinking, habits, or environments that contributed to your brokenness. God does His part in restoring you, but now you must do your part in stewarding the restoration.

> **"Let us walk honestly, as in the day... put ye on the Lord Jesus Christ, and make not provision for the flesh..." — Romans 13:13–14 (KJV)**

Restoration is not fragile, but it must be honored. The renewed walk requires new choices, fresh boundaries, and surrendered obedience.

A RENEWED WALK REFLECTS A RENEWED MIND

God's restoration begins in the heart, but it continues in the mind. To walk renewed, your thought life must align with your new identity in Christ. You cannot think like a prisoner if you've been set free.

> **"And be not conformed to this world: but be ye transformed by the renewing of your mind..." — Romans 12:2 (KJV)**

A renewed mind leads to a transformed life. What you believe about yourself post-restoration determines how you behave. Do you still see yourself as broken? Or do you see yourself as beloved, whole, and commissioned?

YOUR WALK BECOMES A WITNESS

Restoration is not only personal—it's missional. How you walk after you've been restored becomes a testimony to others. When people see your life radiating peace, purpose, and power, they become curious about the God who restored you.

> **"Let your light so shine before men, that they may see your good works, and glorify your Father which is in heaven." — Matthew 5:16 (KJV)**

Living restored means walking in visible fruitfulness. Others will see that what tried to destroy you did not have the final say.

STAY IN STEP WITH THE SPIRIT

Walking renewed is not about striving—it's about abiding. The Holy Spirit now leads your life, not pain, fear, or performance. The pace of your walk must match the pace of His voice.

"If we live in the Spirit, let us also walk in the Spirit." — Galatians 5:25 (KJV)

This is daily, intimate obedience. Sometimes the Spirit will lead you back into hard places to bring healing to others. Other times, He'll lead you into seasons of stillness. Living restored means trusting His leadership over your preferences.

RESTORATION IS SUSTAINED BY GRATITUDE

One of the greatest weapons to sustain your walk in wholeness is thankfulness. Gratitude roots you in the present and guards your heart from returning to past bondage.

"Bless the Lord, O my soul, and forget not all his benefits: Who forgiveth all thine iniquities; who healeth all thy diseases... who crowneth thee with lovingkindness and tender mercies." — Psalm 103:2–4 (KJV)

A grateful heart remembers what God has done and stays aligned with what God is doing. It keeps you moving forward, not looking back.

REFLECTION

- Are you living like someone who has been fully restored?

- In what ways is your renewed walk influencing others?

- What daily practices help you stay aligned with the Spirit and anchored in gratitude?

SCRIPTURE REFERENCES

- Romans 13:13–14
- Romans 12:2
- Matthew 5:16
- Galatians 5:25
- Psalm 103:2–4

CONCLUSION

BEYOND RECOGNITION—A TESTIMONY OF HIS POWER

Restoration is not about returning to the version of you that existed before the storm, the fall, the wilderness, or the pain. It's about becoming someone unrecognizable in the best way—transformed by the power of God, marked by mercy, and filled with a strength you didn't have before. When God restores, He doesn't take you back—He takes you forward, beyond recognition.

You are not just the healed version of who you were. You are the redeemed, refined, and recommissioned version of who God always intended you to be.

YOU WILL NOT LOOK LIKE WHAT YOU'VE BEEN THROUGH

When God finishes His work in your life, people will wonder how you made it. They'll ask how you recovered, how you kept your mind, how you found joy again. You will carry no scent of the fire, no sign of the pit, and no residue of shame.

"And the princes, governors, and captains, and the king's counsellors, being gathered together, saw these men, upon whose bodies the fire had no power, nor was an hair of their

head singed, neither were their coats changed, nor the smell of fire had passed on them." — Daniel 3:27 (KJV)

Like the Hebrew boys in Babylon, you'll come out of the fire without evidence of the trauma—only evidence of the testimony. That's restoration beyond recognition.

YOUR LIFE BECOMES EVIDENCE OF GOD'S GLORY

God's restoration work in your life is not just for you—it's for His glory. People won't see your past; they'll see His power. They won't dwell on what you lost; they'll marvel at what God rebuilt.

"This people have I formed for myself; they shall shew forth my praise." — Isaiah 43:21 (KJV)

Your life becomes a stage where heaven's glory is displayed. Your scars become sermons. Your deliverance becomes a declaration.

RESTORATION UNLOCKS A GREATER CALLING

After Peter denied Jesus, he was not disqualified. Instead, Jesus restored him and recommissioned him.

"Feed my sheep… follow me." — John 21:17, 19 (KJV)

Peter was restored not to his former place, but to a greater one. The man who once crumbled in fear would later stand boldly on the day of Pentecost and preach a message that brought 3,000 souls to Christ. Restoration doesn't return you to old levels—it ushers you into divine assignment.

YOU WERE ALWAYS MEANT TO RISE AGAIN

The enemy may have written your obituary, but heaven had already scheduled your comeback. Nothing about your fall, delay, trauma, or brokenness caught God off guard. He already factored your failure into your future.

> **"Rejoice not against me, O mine enemy: when I fall, I shall arise..." — Micah 7:8 (KJV)**

This is not just about getting back up. It's about rising into a restored identity, walking in renewed authority, and living out a redemptive destiny.

YOU ARE THE TESTIMONY

You don't have to preach a sermon to declare God's power—you are the sermon. Every step you take in peace, joy, faith, and purpose is proof that the hand of God has been on your life. You are the living, breathing evidence that restoration is real, and Jesus still makes all things new.

> **"And they overcame him by the blood of the Lamb, and by the word of their testimony..." — Revelation 12:11 (KJV)**

Let your life speak. Let your restoration declare to the world: *"Yes, I was broken. But I am restored. And I don't look like what I've been through—I look like who He called me to be."*

FINAL REFLECTION

- What part of your story has become your testimony?

- Are you ready to fully embrace the "beyond recognition" version of yourself?

- Who in your life needs to see that restoration is still possible?

CLOSING DECLARATION

"I am no longer who I was. I am who God has called me to be. My past is not my identity. My restoration is complete. My life is a testimony of His mercy, grace, and power. I walk forward renewed, repurposed, and restored—beyond recognition."

www.ingramcontent.com/pod-product-compliance
Lightning Source LLC
LaVergne TN
LVHW021548080426
835509LV00019B/2899